WITHDRAWN

SAWDUST
THE AMAZING LIFE

BY RALPH COVERT AND G. RILEY MILLS

AND **SPANGLES** OF W.C. COUP

ILLUSTRATED BY GISELLE POTTER

Abrams Books for Young Readers, New York

MANY YEARS AGO, IN A TINY INDIANA TOWN, there lived a small boy with big dreams. His name was William Cameron Coup. His father ran a humble tavern, where William would help out any way he could. But he quickly grew bored with hauling garbage and sweeping floors. Like most young boys, he longed for adventure and excitement.

One day he passed a sign that caught his attention. The circus was coming to town!

WITNESS THE WONDER AND THE

That night William stepped into a dream world. Music filled the air. Colors danced before his eyes. He saw candy butchers selling the sweetest of treats: popcorn, taffy, and gingerbread.

William made his way into the big tent. Inside he saw lions and elephants and a giraffe as tall as a tree! There was a tightrope walker, acrobats on horseback, and even a strongman who could break steel chains with his bare hands!

And clowns who made him laugh so hard his sides hurt!

William instantly fell in love with the sights and sounds of the big top, and it was at that moment that he made a decision that would change his life forever: He decided to run away with the circus!

Life in the circus was hard work and long hours, but William loved every moment of it. Even the time he fell asleep in Old Romeo the elephant's cage and awoke hanging upside down from his trunk!

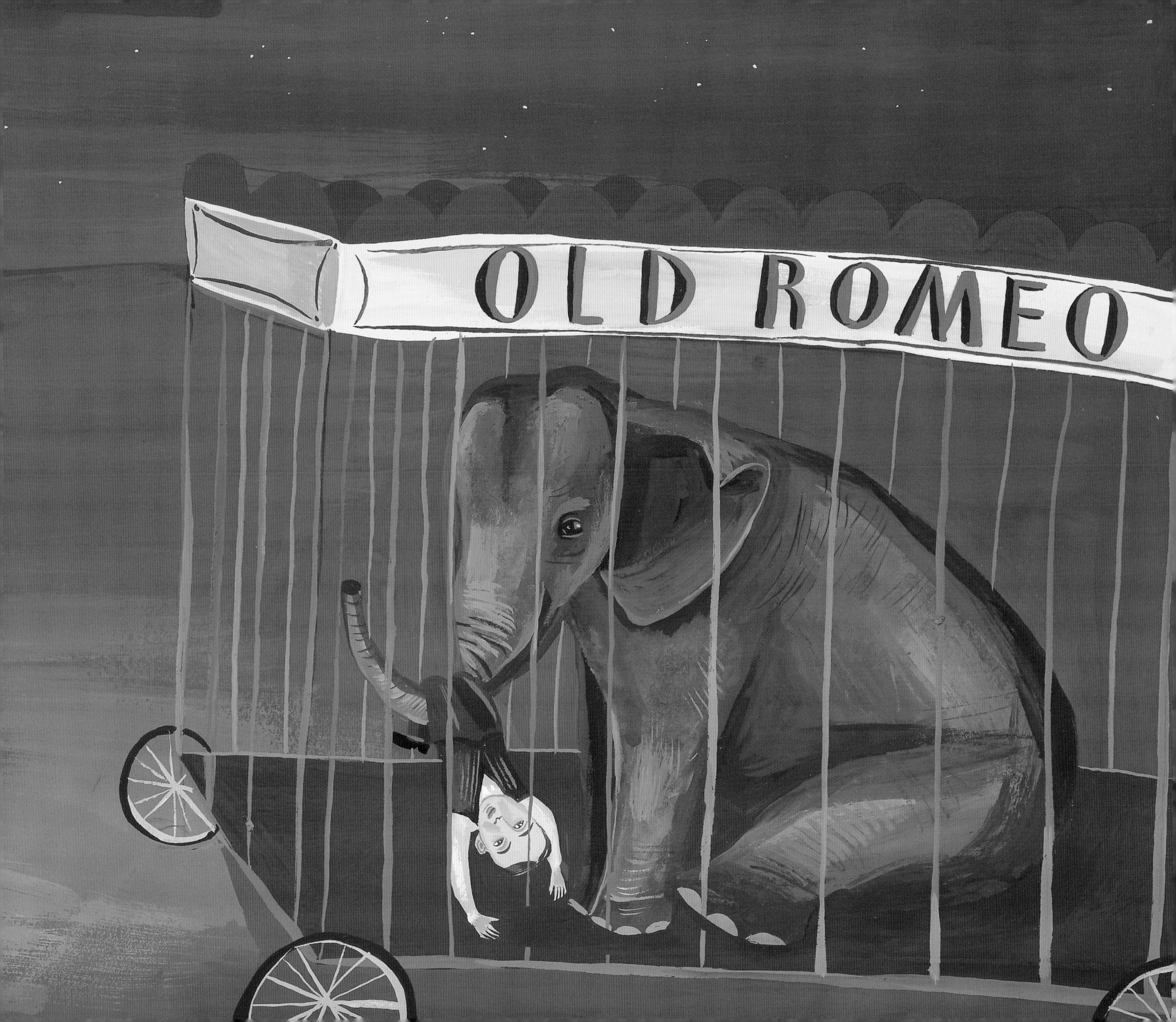
OLD ROMEO

A caravan of horse-drawn wagons would move the entire circus from one town to the next, usually at night, when the performers and animals were fast asleep. Dawn was when the canvasmen would set to work—hoisting poles, hammering stakes, and raising the colorful canvas of the big tent. As William grew older and stronger, they let him help, swinging the big sledgehammer and joining in their traditional chant: *"Heave it, heavy down! Hump back, jump back! Take it back, break your back! Down stake: Next!"*

Years passed, and William grew into a young man. Circus life was in his blood—he had found his true home. Eventually, he came to run his very own circus. Like all good showmen, he needed a name that could be printed on posters and banners, something with style: He would call himself W.C. Coup.

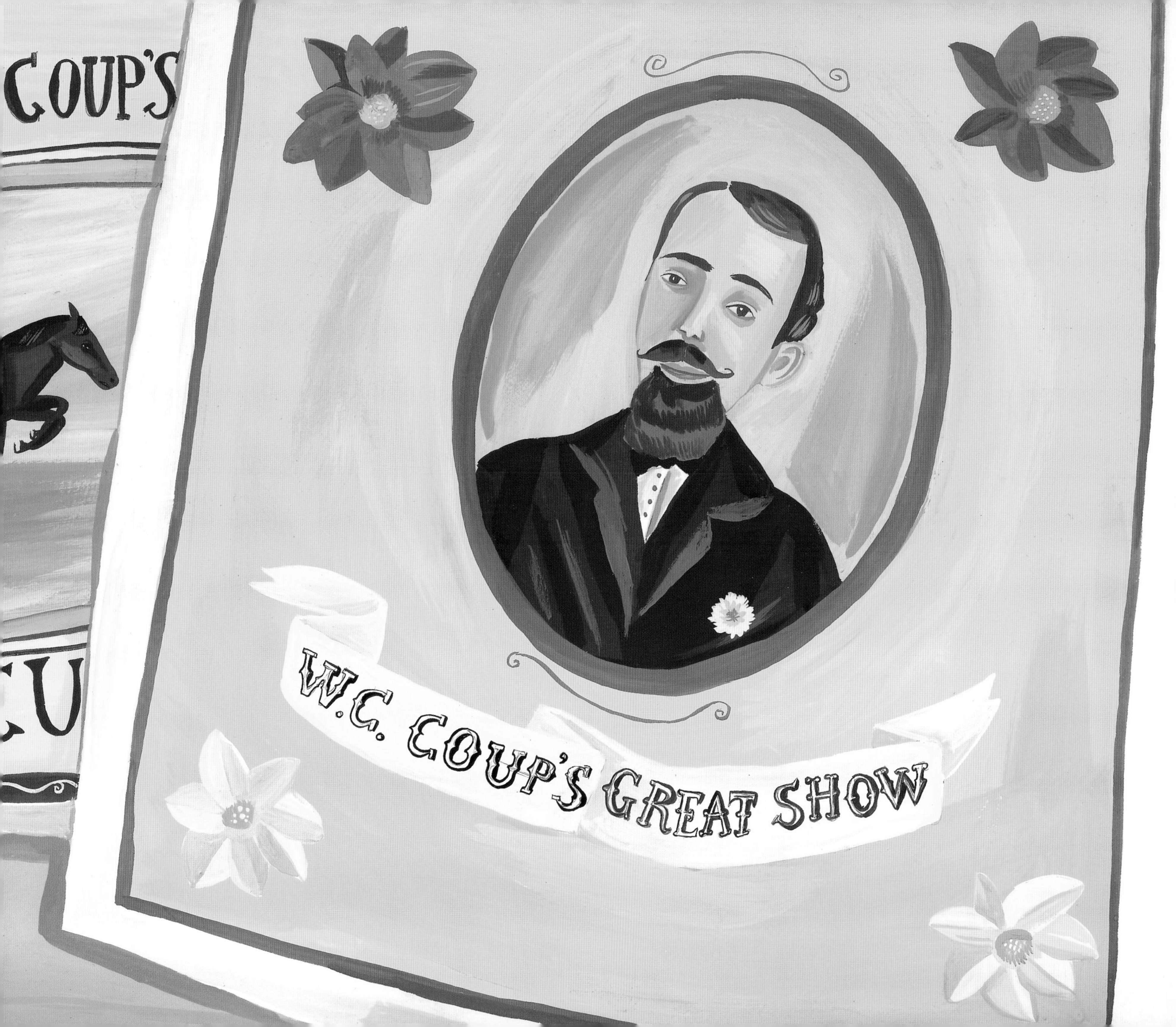
COUP'S
CU
W.C. COUP'S GREAT SHOW

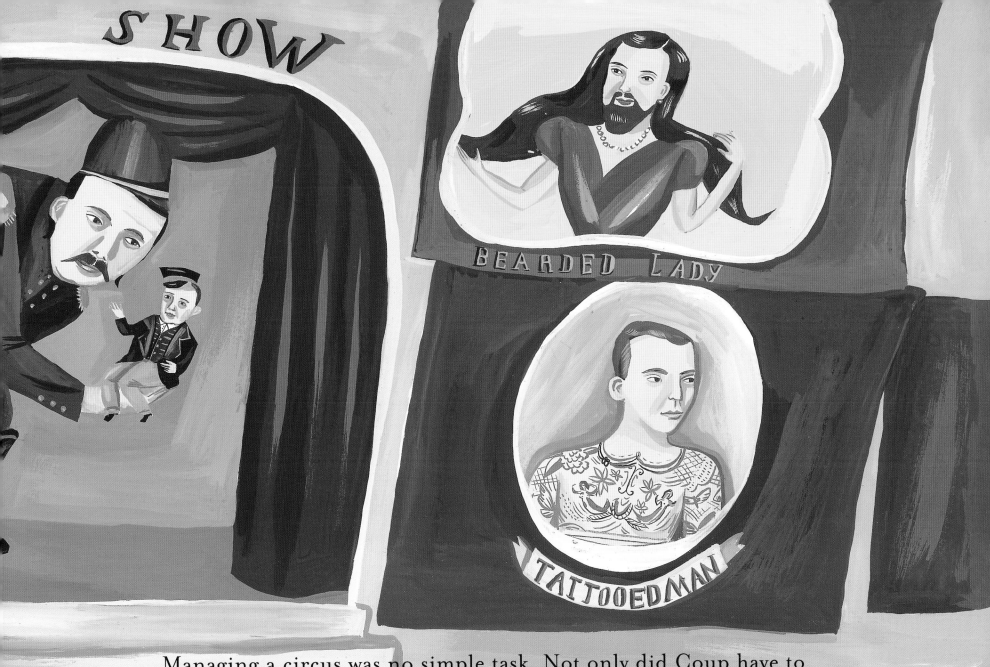

Managing a circus was no simple task. Not only did Coup have to keep track of the ticket sellers, the performers, and all the animals, but he also had to oversee the sideshow, which was filled with many strange and interesting sights. Coup's favorite was General Tom Thumb, a man so small he could sit in the palm of your hand!

But Coup's star attraction by
far was Dan Rice, the King of Clowns.
Rice was the most famous circus performer in
America—the only person in circus history ever to
present a tightrope-walking elephant! And he had even
performed for President Abraham Lincoln himself! Crowds
adored the clown's comic songs and speeches, and his unique
and colorful costume was said to be the model for Uncle Sam.

Often, Coup would stand in a dark corner of the big tent, watching the wonder of the circus. With the piles of sawdust at his feet and spangles glittering in front of his eyes, he would admire his creation and dream big dreams.

Coup loved the animals in his circus and stocked his menagerie with the help of a man named Charles Reiche. Reiche would travel for months to the deepest wilds of Africa, capturing exotic animals and transporting them back across the ocean by boat. It was difficult, dangerous work, but Reiche loved the thrill of the hunt.

For W.C. Coup, the show life *was* his life, and the people and animals in the circus had become his family. And that suited him just fine.

One day a telegram arrived from the famous showman
P.T. Barnum. He asked Coup to come to New York City
to be his partner. Together, they could create the most
dazzling circus the world had ever seen. It was the chance
of a lifetime. Coup packed his bags and said good-bye to
the old-time wagon circus. He was off to the big city!

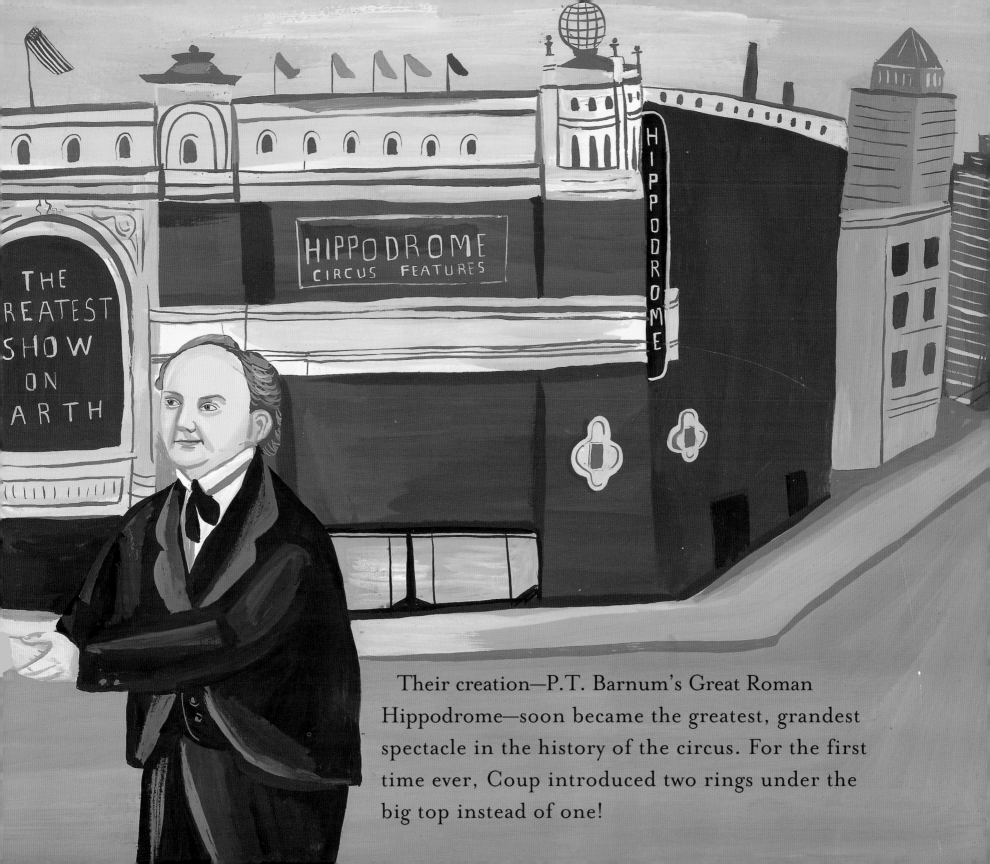

Their creation—P.T. Barnum's Great Roman Hippodrome—soon became the greatest, grandest spectacle in the history of the circus. For the first time ever, Coup introduced two rings under the big top instead of one!

But he wasn't finished yet. He had even bigger plans:
Why not take this massive show on the road? By train, no
less! And so Coup's idea of the circus train forever
changed how the circus traveled.

THE W.C. COUP CIRCUS

While on the road, Coup met with his old friend Charles Reiche, who presented him with plans for a new business venture, the likes of which had never been seen before: an aquarium, full of rare marine treasures from around the world! A museum of aquatic wonder. A circus underwater!

They set to work on Coup's biggest dream yet—and his biggest gamble—scouring the globe for the most unique and fascinating sea creatures they could find: devilfish, sea otters, toadfish, scallops, starfish, lobsters, porpoises, sharks. No expense was spared—they even transported a whale in the cargo hold of a ship!

The aquarium itself was a massive brick
structure filled with tanks of iron and glass.
There were pumps and pipes everywhere, moving water in and out of
the towering crystal cages. Golden light streamed in from the skylights
above. Day after day, Coup watched with awe as his creation took shape.

At last, it was finished—the New York Aquarium was ready to open its doors to the public! Crowds packed the streets of New York City in the thousands, anxiously awaiting their first glimpse of this fantastic underwater wonderland! Oh, and the sights they saw inside! A full orchestra filled the grand hall with music as people rushed from one tank to the next, feasting their eyes upon these most curious of creatures. Living monsters from the depths of the ocean! Alligators, squid, sea lions, hellbenders, kingio, sea anemones, tigerfish, porgies, pike, sturgeon, stingrays, crawfish, dogfish, sea horses, sea urchins, eels.

The aquarium was a success, and Coup was called a hero. He was never so proud in his whole life.

Often, at night, when the crowds had finally gone home, Coup would remain in the aquarium, alone. There, bathed in the soft blue light of the tanks, he would admire his creation. If you had been there to see him, you might have wondered if the twinkle in his eye was a reflection of the fish in the tanks, or the glimmer of yet another dream waiting to come out.

Because for W.C. Coup, there was always a bigger dream to be found.

Author's Note

When we first stumbled upon W.C. Coup's out-of-print memoirs in the archives of a college research library, we were immediately drawn to his story, both because of the colorful circus world he lived in and because of the amazing things he accomplished. Following Coup as he moved from one adventure to the next, we realized his life was a spectacle paralleling and reflecting the grandeur of the circus itself.

We chose to end this telling of Coup's story with his dream fulfilled and his heart content. There was, however, a final twist after the spectacular opening of the New York Aquarium. Coup and his partner, Charles Reiche, became embroiled in a bitter dispute over business details and promises they'd made, promises that Coup insisted on honoring over Reiche's objections. Eventually, the two men chose to flip a penny to decide ownership of the aquarium. Imagine that today—two grown men willing to risk their life's fortune on the toss of a coin! When Coup lost the bet, he walked away from his beloved creation forever, his pockets empty. But he dreamed again, built again, and soared again, eventually opening a traveling show called the New United Monster Shows, which featured trained horses, Lulu the Human Cannonball, an entire tribe of Zulu warriors, and a troupe of Japanese acrobats. The show ultimately became one of the largest consolidated circuses in the United States. Later he put together various Wild West and trained-animal exhibitions and created the Enchanted Rolling Palaces—elaborate museums housed on trains. Truly, Coup was a man of great passion and purpose, which is why we felt his story was one that needed to be told, to remind us all that the extraordinary is waiting inside all of us, all the time.

For Fiona, Rita, Jayme, and Abby
—R.C.

For my girls—Jo, Sadie, and Sawyer
—G.R.M.

For Isabel and Pia
—G.P.

Library of Congress Cataloging-in-Publication Data:

Covert, Ralph.
Sawdust and spangles : the amazing life of W.C. Coup / Ralph Covert, G. Riley
Mills ; [illustrations by] Giselle Potter.
p. cm.
ISBN-13: 978-0-8109-9351-8
ISBN-10: 0-8109-9351-1
1. Coup, W. C. (William Cameron), 1857–1895. 2. Circus owners—United
States—Biography. 3. Circus—United States.
I. Mills, G. Riley. II. Title.

GV1811.C66C67 2007
791.3092—dc22
[B]
2006031981

Text copyright © 2007 Ralph Covert and G. Riley Mills
Illustrations copyright © 2007 Giselle Potter

Book design by Chad W. Beckerman

Published in 2007 by Abrams Books for Young Readers,
an imprint of Harry N. Abrams, Inc.

Printed and bound in China
10 9 8 7 6 5 4 3 2 1

HNA ▮▮▮▮▮
harry n. abrams, inc.
a subsidiary of La Martinière Groupe
115 West 18th Street
New York, NY 10011
WWW.HNABOOKS.COM